BONNIE PRINCE CHARLIE

FRONT COVER: *Prince Charles Edward Stuart by Louis-Gabriel Blanchet; an early indication of the elegant, confident young man who was to charm his way beyond history into legend.*

RIGHT: *Bonnie Prince Charlie as his supporters saw him. This was painted between 1739 and 1745 and shows Charles with a red tartan jacket wearing the Star and Ribbon of the Garter. On his blue bonnet he wears a white cockade, symbol of the House of Stuart.*

BACK COVER: *The de jure King of Scotland, England and Ireland. This portrait by H. D. Hamilton shows Charles aged 55. According to Jacobite sentiment he had been Charles III since his father's death in 1766. A less regal portrait would be difficult to imagine. The contagious charm and the good looks have gone. Instead an unfulfilled old man stares out pensively from the portrait.*

BONNIE PRINCE CHARLIE

ALAN BOLD

ON the last night of 1720 Charles Edward Louis Philip Casimir Stuart was born prince of Wales—in a borrowed papal palazzo in Rome. By the Stuart doctrine of divine right he should have inherited more than a title but the tactless arrogance of his grandfather James II had lost a kingdom, and the pious diffidence of his father James Francis Edward Stuart had failed to win it back.

It was James II's insistence on his divine right to reinstate Catholicism that disarmed his Tory friends and alienated his Whig critics. When, in controversial circumstances, he produced a male heir he precipitated the bloodless English Revolution of 1688 which brought William and Mary to power as constitutional monarchs. James II's defeat at the battle of the Boyne, 1689, left him a mere *de jure* monarch and when he died in 1701, a

pensioner of Louis XIV, his son James Francis Edward was proclaimed king of England, Scotland and Ireland in France but ignored in Great Britain. Instead, on William III's death six months after James's, it was Anne—William's sister-in-law and James Francis Edward's stepsister—who became *de facto* monarch.

James Francis Edward, the old Pretender, made three attempts to regain his kingdom. In 1708 his small fleet was ignominiously dismissed in the Firth of Forth by admiral Byng. Stirred by the waves of unrest following the Hanoverian Succession 'Jamie the Rover' tried again in 1715. This time he was proclaimed king at Braemar by the earl of Mar who subsequently contrived to lose the battle of Sherriffmuir while the English Jacobites fell at Preston. In 1719 James made a third attempt, but the Spanish armada promised him

was destroyed by storm and a planned Scottish diversion inevitably collapsed at the pass of Glenshiel.

Though James was a courageous man he was modest and uninspiring. Concerned with his record of failure important Jacobites reminded James of his obligation to produce a Stuart heir. On their advice James agreed to marry the 17-year-old princess Clementina Sobieski of Poland, first by proxy then in person on 1 September, 1719. The birth of his first son in 1720 was warmly acclaimed in Jacobite circles as a major achievement. Still only 32 the Pretender could reasonably hope for great things from his son. He took personal charge of Charles's development and to obviate the family's religious handicap provided a Protestant tutor as well as the Irish Catholic Sir Thomas Sheridan.

Charles's physical progress was precocious. He was athletically inclined, wiry and tough, and soon became an enthusiastic golfer, an accomplished shot, and an expert with the crossbow. When Charles was about seven the duke of Liria claimed to have "seen him take a crossbow and kill birds on the roof, and split a rolling ball with a bolt ten times in succession". Little wonder that Liria considered Charles to be "the most ideal Prince I have ever met in the course of my life". Whig propaganda often implied that Charles was an infirm, lethargic child, but a letter from the 8-year-old Prince to his father reveals an obstreperous, mischievous boy. "I will be very dutifull to Mama", he writes, "and not jump too near her".

Unlike his brother Henry, born in 1725, Charles was never academically outstanding. His spelling was atrocious (as late as 1744 he wrote "Gems" for James) but he used the spoken word with considerable dramatic effect expressing himself fluently in Italian, French, Spanish and English. Apart from dancing, his greatest leisure activity was music. He played the violin well and often.

Instinctively, though, Charles

*   *   *

FACING PAGE: *The parents of Prince Charles. James Francis Edward Stuart, The Old Pretender (1688–1766), (left), a portrait by Trevasini showing James at the time of his first expedition in 1708. His birth to James II and Mary of Modena in 1688—contested by the Whigs who claimed he had been smuggled in by warming pan—seemed to guarantee the Catholic succession and provoked the English Revolution. In exile, James spent 25 years in France and after the abortive 1715 rebellion found asylum in Rome and married Princess Sobieski of Poland (right). She was chosen for her beauty, maternal connections and vast fortune. George II tried in vain to stop the marriage and arranged her detention in Austria, but Charles Wogan, an Irish Jacobite, smuggled her into Italy where she married James by proxy in 1719. Clementina soon tired of the sham court and resented Charles's Protestant tutor. Soon after her second son, Henry, was born, she retired to a convent and remained there until shortly before her death in 1735.*

RIGHT: *Prince Charles Edward Stuart. This portrait was painted in 1732 by Antonio David.*

wished to express himself physically. In 1734, when he was 13, the duke of Liria came to the Palazzo Muti on his way to join Don Carlos's Spanish army at Gaeta, where Austrian Imperialist forces were making a last attempt to save Naples. Charles not only accompanied Liria to the besieged sea-port but joined him in the front-line trenches. "Neither the noise of cannon", Liria recorded, "nor the hiss of bullets could produce any sign of fear in him".

When Gaeta surrendered Charles joined Don Carlos on his triumphant march to Naples. Already his manner and conversation were so "bewitching", according to Liria, that he impressed the rank-and-file soldiers as much as the king of Naples. This personal charm was demonstrated again when, after the death of his mother in 1735,

Charles left the Palazzo Muti on a grand tour of the northern Italian cities. He was rapturously received to the intense indignation of the British Government.

Although intent on a military career British pressure prevented any European army accepting him. So Charles spent his late teens going on long hill walks and shooting expeditions when he was not involved in prolonged musical sessions. Increasingly frustrated at fiddling while the Jacobite Cause smouldered Charles must have been elated by the outbreak of the War of the Austrian Succession (1740–48). In any European conflict, however peripherally it affected Britain and France, there was a possibility that the Stuarts would be used to embarrass the British Government and divide public opinion. When

Continued on page 5

Britain entered the war, in 1743, George II personally led his army to victory over a superior French force at Dettingen. Louis XV was furious enough to plan, simultaneously, a French invasion of England and an uprising in Scotland. Charles was accordingly summoned to Paris.

By March 1744, Charles was waiting

*   *   *

LEFT: *Prince Charles Edward Stuart and the Irish Jacobite Antoine Walsh, on the shores of Loch Nan Uamh* (Loch of the Caves). *On 26 July 1745, Charles and his seven men of Moidart landed here on the Scottish mainland between Moidart and Arisaig. He had been brought from France in Walsh's frigate* la Doutelle.

ABOVE: *Glenfinnan. In this secluded narrow glen at the head of Loch Shiel, Charles raised the Standard of the House of Stuart on 19 August 1745. The column and statue of a Highlander was erected in 1815 by Alexander Macdonald of Glenladale, descendant of a devoted Jacobite.*

at the fishing town of Gravelines while at Dunkirk the celebrated Marshal Maurice de Saxe prepared 15,000 troops for an invasion of the Thames. Unfortunately the weather, that constant enemy of the Stuarts, intervened: a wildly destructive storm smashed the French fleet at Dunkirk. There would be no invasion.

Charles's hopes survived the storm intact. When he realised the French were now reluctant to help him he borrowed 180,000 livres (£4,000) on the strength of the Sobieski rubies and bought broadswords, field-pieces, muskets and ammunition. Two Jacobite shipowners supplied him with transport: Antoine Walsh provided a 110-ton, 16-gun frigate *la Doutelle*; and Walter Routledge offered the *Elisabeth*, a 64-gun man-of-war, as escort. Charles had determined that he would not face a lifetime of begging for French help, nor would he return to his father's make-believe court in Rome. If necessary he would start an uprising on his own.

This was, almost literally, to be the case. His military hardware hardly

constituted an adequate instrument with which to ensure the restoration of the house of Stuart. His seven elderly companions (to become known as the Seven Men of Moidart from that area on the Scottish mainland) could never comprise a fighting force. Among the Seven were Sir Thomas Sheridan, his former tutor; colonel John William O'Sullivan, a notorious Irish soldier-of-fortune; and Aeneas Macdonald, a Scottish-born Paris banker with useful contacts in Highland Scotland. All Charles really had was an absolute and unshakeable conviction in the justice of the Stuart cause and an ability to present his case eloquently to others.

On 5 July, 1745 Charles, disguised as a divinity student, boarded *la Doutelle* and set off on the 18-day journey to Scotland. On the fifth day at sea, off the Lizard, his ships were attacked by a British man-of-war the *Lion*. After an exchange of fire the *Elisabeth* drove the British ship away. However, her own losses were so considerable that she had to return to Brest. Charles was asked to do the same.

Continued on page 6

Instead he continued the journey, on his unescorted frigate, through storms and dangerous enemy sightings until finally, on 23 July, he reached the silver beach on the little Hebridean island of Briskay. Before they landed an eagle was seen hovering above *la Doutelle* and one of the Prince's men remarked "The king of birds is come to welcome Your Royal Highness on your arrival in Scotland". Although poetically apt the eagle's lead was not to be immediately followed by the sceptical Highland chiefs.

Charles sheltered in a fisherman's hut choking as some flounders were roasted on an open fire. As he was on Clanranald territory he sent for

★   ★   ★

ABOVE LEFT: *Donald Cameron, Young Lochiel (1695–1748). The 50-year-old chief of the 800 strong Cameron clan was persuaded against his better judgment to join Charles in 1745. Without Lochiel's commitment to the cause it is doubtful that Charles could have raised the Standard. Thereafter Lochiel became one of the prince's most selfless and devoted supporters. He took Edinburgh and at Culloden was badly wounded in both legs. Rather than flee Scotland after this battle he waited for the prince and sailed with him to France on L'Heureux. He died later in exile.*

BELOW LEFT: *Charles's 'Medusa Head' targe. This shield, covered in leather and embossed in silver is fine 18th-century French work and was made and presented to the prince by his admirers in Paris prior to his departure for Scotland in 1745.*

FACING PAGE: *Lord George Murray (1694–1760). Perhaps the most controversial figure of the '45, Lord George was exiled for his involvement in the 1715 uprising and was eventually pardoned through the influence of his father the duke of Atholl. Charles appointed him his lieutenant-general in 1745 but was openly suspicious of him. Not allowed to negotiate the capitulation of Carlisle he resigned and Charles only reinstated him under pressure from the army. At Derby he insisted on retreat and Charles never forgave him. However, he was a competent, often brilliant, military tactitian. He excelled at Prestonpans and organised the victory at Falkirk. After Culloden he wrote criticising the prince severely and when he arrived in Rome in 1747 Charles asked his father to place this 'Divill' under house arrest but James refused. Later when Lord George tried to see the prince in Paris he was threatened and told to leave. He died in exile in Holland.*

Macdonald of Boisdale who arrived promptly the next morning. His reaction to the absurdly ambitious project was simple and direct. He told Charles to go home. "I am come home, sir" replied the Prince. Then, though he was a total stranger to Scotland, added that "my faithful Highlanders will stand by me". Boisdale disagreed, predicting that the planned uprising would fail.

This was certainly realistic. Logically Charles had no chance of success. With no prospect or promise of French help he faced a stable kingdom reconciled (as it had not been in 1715) to the House of Hanover. Even the Tories appreciated the commercial prosperity achieved by Walpole's premiership, and Lowland Scotland was flourishing on the European trade made possible by the Union of 1707. As for the "faithful Highlanders" Charles had been told, before he even left France, that "he could not positively depend upon more than 4,000 Highlanders, if so many". For all that Charles felt his timing was right.

On 25 July Charles and his Seven Men sailed for the mainland, anchoring in Loch nan Uamh between Moidart and Arisaig, then establishing a base at Borrodale in Arisaig. His initial request for Highland support being rejected Charles was left with a clear choice: to make an impressive personal impact or to return to Europe. If he could only secure the help of Donald Cameron of Lochiel, influential head of the Cameron Clan, he would have made an auspicious beginning. Although warned by his brother to deal with Charles in writing, because "if this Prince once sets his eyes upon you he will make you do whatever he pleases", Lochiel decided to put his objections in private interview.

He criticised Charles for arriving without French support. He suggested a propitious return to Europe with the object of arranging a properly armed invasion. He counselled the Prince to "be more temperate". Showing all his theatrical gifts Charles delivered a crushing psychological counterpunch. "In a few days", he told Lochiel, "with the few friends that I have, I will erect the Royal Standard, and proclaim to the people of Britain that Charles Stuart is come over to claim the crown of his ancestors, to win it, or perish in the attempt. Lochiel, who, as my father has often told me, was our firmest friend, may stay at home,

and learn from the newspapers the fate of his Prince". It was too much for Lochiel. "No, I'll share the fate of my Prince", he replied. Then, speaking with the absolute power of the territorial chieftain, added "and so shall every man over whom nature or fortune hath given me any power".

This crucial conversion set a stirring example for the other Clans. Charles sent away *la Doutelle*, thus ostentatiously stranding himself in Scotland. "The worst that can happen to me", he wrote his father, "is to die at the head of such brave people as I find here". Already this handsome, dark-eyed, 25-year-old Prince was consciously assuming legendary proportions.

Convinced he had enough backing to raise the Standard Charles travelled, by way of Glenladale, to the vale of Glenfinnan at the head of Loch Sheil. It was 11 a.m. on 19 August. Charles wore a brown coat over scarlet breeches and waistcoat. Expecting a massive gathering of the Clans he found only 150 Clanranalds. After three hours he was clearly agitated and disappointed. Then, in the distance, he heard bagpipes playing the Cameron war pibroch. Slowly and impressively 700 Camerons came into view with Lochiel at their head. It was enough for Charles. On the flat ground at the head of the loch the red and white silk standard of the House of Stuart was raised. James was proclaimed king and Charles was appointed regent. A manifesto lamented

Continued on page 9

ABOVE: *Duddingston Loch and village from Holyrood Park. Charles established an army camp in the village during his six weeks' stay in Edinburgh. He held court at Holyrood and usually spent the evening with his men in Duddingston.*

★

LEFT: *Edinburgh Castle. Although the Jacobites occupied the city for six weeks they never succeeded in taking the castle.*

★

FACING PAGE: *The palace of Holyroodhouse, Edinburgh. Charles entered the 15th-century royal residence on 17 September 1745. After his victory at Prestonpans, Charles held court at the palace for six weeks, for he needed this time to add to his army, but it also gave the English government time to recall troops from Flanders.*

★   ★   ★

If you are interested in Scotland and Scottish history, the following titles are published by Pitkins: *Mary Queen of Scots*; *Robert Burns*; *City of Edinburgh*. Also to be published in the near future, *Scottish Clans* and *Scottish Tartans*.

8

the fact that Scotland had been "reduced to the condition of a province, under the specious pretence of an union"; declared a general pardon; guaranteed a free parliament and religious freedom; and concluded with a promise to "advance trade, to relieve the poor, and establish the general welfare and tranquillity of the nation". These popular sentiments were followed by a short speech by Charles. Cheers filled the glen. The prince had come home.

More clansmen arrived; three hundred Keppoch Macdonalds; some Macleods. Eventually there were around 1,200. Charles was euphoric. He had raised the Standard as he had said he would. In Edinburgh Scotland's commander-in-chief Sir John Cope took him seriously enough to leave the capital intent on battle. A proclamation was issued offering a reward of £30,000 "to such person or persons who shall so seize and secure the said son of the said pretender, so that he may be brought to justice". At last Bonnie Prince Charlie was a wanted man.

The newly proclaimed Regent took his Highland army to the Corrieyarrick Pass to encounter Cope. He adopted Highland dress and mixed freely with the clansmen occasionally dropping a few recently acquired Gaelic phrases. Though they were soon ready to die for him there was to be no battle yet. Cope was shrewd enough to realise that a mountain pass would be too advantageous to the Highlanders, so he turned north to Inverness. Charles and his men marched through the Corrieyarrick Pass and though they were disappointed at Cope's reluctance to fight realised they had an open route, through Atholl country, to Edinburgh.

At Garvamore they seized Evan Macpherson of Cluny whose conversion to the Cause eventually added about 400 Macphersons to the Highland army. At Perth Charles appointed the duke of Perth and Lord George Murray joint Lieutenant Generals. O'Sullivan, one of the Seven Men of Moidart, became quartermaster-general. While Lord George prepared the Highland army at Perth, Cope moved to Aberdeen anxious to sail to Leith and defend Edinburgh.

From Perth the Highlanders went by way of Stirling and Linlithgow to Corstorphine, outside Edinburgh. Rather than face this inexorable advance Government dragoons kept retreating. At Corstorphine Charles sent an ultimatum demanding the surrender of Edinburgh with the warning that "if any opposition be made to us, we cannot answer for the consequences". A nocturnal deputation from the town council, well aware that Cope had landed at Dunbar, asked for more time. Charles refused to see them let alone bargain with them, and was furious at Lord George for supporting their request. Lochiel and his Camerons were sent to take the city as peacefully as possible. About 2 a.m. on 17 September the Netherbow Port gate opened to let the deputation's coach back to the stables in the Connongate. Instantly the screaming Camerons, with broadswords and targes at the ready, rushed through the gate, up the High Street, and into Parliament Close. By 6 a.m. the whole city, apart from the Castle, was theirs. Edinburgh awoke to the sound of pipes and the sight of white cockades on Highland bonnets. Charles himself spent the night at his camp in Duddingston. In the morning he rode into King's Park and dismounted at St. Anthony's Well to gaze at the captured city. Staring back were masses of curious citizens anxious for a glimpse of the victorious prince in his tartan short-coat. He too wore the blue bonnet and white cockade. To avoid the over enthusiastic clamour of the crowd he remounted, rode to the palace of Holyroodhouse and reappeared at the windows to acknowledge his people. It was a great moment for him. One month after Glenfinnan he was in command of the Scottish capital.

If he was to consolidate his position he would have to deal with Cope who had landed at Dunbar with 500 cavalry, 2,000 infantry and artillery. Charles had 50 horse, 2,500 infantry, but all the artillery he had was an archaic field-piece, "the mother of Muskets", to which the Highlanders had become sentimentally attached. Still, their march from Duddingston was confident enough.

After resting in a field Charles decided to attack at daybreak, taking up a local offer to show his men over the marshy bog to the battlefield at Prestonpans. At 3 a.m. 21 September, they silently moved in a thick mist which hid them until they were ready to attack Cope's red-coated infantrymen. The Jacobite right wing was commanded by the Duke of Perth (with the Macdonalds in their traditional place on the right), the centre by Malcolm Macgregor, and the Cameronian left-wing by Lord George. Whereas Charles told his men victory would make them "a free and happy people" Cope contemptuously dismissed his opponents as "a parcel of rabble, a small number of Highlanders, a parcel of brutes".

These "brutes" had a secret weapon in the ferocious Highland charge: a pre-emptive strike of such intensity that it inflicted terror as well as destruction on the enemy. Advancing three-deep the Highlanders rapidly broke into small clan units led by well-armed chiefs. With a targe on their left arm, a dirk in the left fist, they rushed forwards firing what muskets they had at close range. Then, drawing their basket-hilted broadswords, they plunged among the enemy.

Such tactics shattered Cope's army in 8 minutes. For a Jacobite loss of 40 men (and 90 wounded) Cope lost hundreds. Charles was magnanimous in victory, preventing a total slaughter —"spare them, they are my father's subjects"—and arranging medical treatment for the wounded of both sides. Cope and his dragoons rushed to bring news of their own defeat to Lord Mark Kerr at Berwick.

After this decisive victory the Highland army, piping *The King shall come into his own again*, were hailed as heroes when they returned to Edinburgh. Charles would have liked to head for London immediately but decided to remain at Edinburgh for reinforcements. During his six weeks at the capital he alternately held court

*   *   *

ABOVE LEFT: *The March to Finchley. Hogarth's engraving shows the English foot guards leaving the Tottenham Court Road turnpike for Finchley where they formed a defensive force. As Hogarth suggests this was a badly trained militia given to drink, yet its existence was one of the arguments used to convince Prince Charles that a retreat from Derby was essential. Having retreated from Derby to the north of England, the Jacobites crossed the border at the river Esk and made their way to Glasgow to try and gain support from this strong anti-Jacobite centre. Having failed they moved north and gained a valuable victory at Falkirk, but crowned this success by wasting valuable time and effort in a futile attempt to capture Stirling Castle (above right).*

at Holyroodhouse and spent evenings with his men at Duddingston. While he expertly performed the role of gracious Regent to the adulation of all (especially the Edinburgh ladies), and while he did swell his ranks, the delay gave George II the opportunity to recall Dutch and English regular troops from Flanders and send them to field-marshal Wade at Newcastle.

Charles felt that "one decisive stroke" was essential and, at a council of war, suggested a sudden attack on Wade followed by a triumphant march to London. Lord George Murray insisted on moving by way of Carlisle, thus avoiding Wade and giving the English and Welsh Jacobites a chance to rally to the cause. Reluctantly Charles agreed to this plan. On 1 November the Highland army of 5,000 foot and 600 cavalry set out for Carlisle in two columns (one cunningly organised by Lord George to convince Wade the Highlanders meant to attack him).

At first the Jacobites had the same kind of success they had experienced in lowland Scotland: they were un-opposed but rather unwelcome. When Carlisle surrendered on 15 November Charles impressively entered the city on a white charger preceded by 100 pipers. With every day his confidence grew, yet while he spent much of his time marching with his men his officers collectively reflected on the surrounding English apathy. It was only at Manchester, which they took on 28 November, that support was substantial enough to produce new recruits—the 300-strong Manchester Regiment. Basically the English were drinking Jacobites, paying lip service to the cause by sipping toasts to "the king over the water". The Stuart Restoration was their enjoyable, self-indulgent romantic fantasy. In fact they preferred the stable reality of established Hanoverian constitutional monarchy to the misty vision of a Stuart return to power. Several of the Chiefs were apprehensive of such lack of support in what was, to them, a foreign country.

At Lichfield, a day's march away, the army of the Duke of Cumberland had gathered. In a brilliant manoeuvre Lord George disguised the intentions of the Jacobite army so skilfully that Cumberland thought they were heading for Wales and accordingly made for Stone. With their route thus cleared the Jacobites reached Derby on 4 December.

Charles now believed his ambitions were about to be fulfilled. He was only 130 miles from London and in command of a confident, unbeaten army of devoted Highlanders. London itself was in a panic. Shops closed up. The bank of England began paying out in sixpences to stop the run on money. George II was ready to return to Hanover. Even the duke of Newcastle, the secretary of state, contemplated a judicious conversion to Jacobitism. At this point, to the amazement of the prince, Lord George Murray advocated retreat.

In a long, bitter council of war on 5 December Lord George put forward his argument. With Cumberland back at Lichfield, Wade at Wetherby, and a large (though badly trained) defence militia at Finchley the 5,000 strong Jacobite army was virtually sur-
Continued on page 15

The battle of Culloden by David Morier. In this vivid impression of the ⟨ ⟩
absorbs the charge of the Camerons, Stewarts and Athollmen. Ja⟨ ⟩

ht on Culloden Moor on 16 April 1746 the red-coated Hanoverian front-line
ners at Southwark were used as models for the Highland charge.

ABOVE LEFT: *The stone on the edge of the battlefield used by the duke of Cumberland to survey the scene as his army defeated the Scottish clans.*

★

ABOVE RIGHT: *Cumberland, who was grossly overweight is seen probably more accurately portrayed in this caricature. He was notoriously insensitive to appeals to humanity and was obsessed by a desire to eliminate the Highland menace. His personal campaign was endorsed by the government who prohibited the use of weapons in the Disarming Act of 1746, and also the wearing of Highland dress. Culloden therefore became a cultural tragedy for Highland Scotland as well as a personal defeat for the Stuart prince.*

★

LEFT: *Culloden Cairn. This great cairn marks the site of the famous battle of Culloden, 1746, when the duke of Cumberland's army crushed the forces of 'Bonnie Prince Charlie' and he lost forever all hope of restoring the Stuart cause.*

★

FACING PAGE: *Old Leanach farmhouse on Culloden muir, said to have been Prince Charles's headquarters during the battle.*

rounded by 30,000 fighting men. The English people were blatantly unsympathetic whereas back in Scotland more men could be raised and an appeal made to France. Charles was astounded. He could see nothing to be gained by retreat: "Rather than go back, I would wish to be twenty feet under ground". He had been brought up to believe that his cause was divinely ordained and his astonishing successes so far only seemed to confirm this. A sudden, fearless strike on London could only bring victory, in his opinion.

Certainly rumours of Highland desertions were grotesquely exaggerated. Certainly there was a reasonable expectation of French, and even Welsh, support if the Highland army reached the British capital. Certainly the Highlanders seemed unbeatable. All posterity can say with certainty is that Charles *might* have been victorious. He was, however, outvoted and had to accept retreat. Furiously he told his council that he felt betrayed. Only humiliation could result from a retreat before "the son of a usurper".

On 6 December, Black Friday for Jacobite hopes, the Highland army began its retreat. Charles, depressed and moody, no longer walked on foot with his men but rode on a black horse. For his part Lord George Murray conducted a retreat every bit as masterly as his advance had been. Commanding the rear-guard he beat off a dragoon attack at Clifton, outside Penrith, so convincingly that Cumberland thought it wise to wait for reinforcements. At Carlisle Charles left a garrison as a base for a possible return to England. On 20 December his army waded 100-abreast through the Esk in full flood. Back on the Scottish side they lit fires and danced to dry themselves out.

An army in retreat does not merit the same respect as an apparently invulnerable force. Whiggish Lowland Scotland was no longer in awe of these tired, uncomprehending Highlanders. Dumfries was hostile. Glasgow, with a 700-strong anti-Jacobite militia to its credit, even more so. Nevertheless Charles spent a week at Glasgow imposing on the citizens the indignity of supplying fresh clothing for his men —including 6,000 Jacobite blue bonnets. A review of his troops on Glasgow Green showed a third of these bonnets to be superfluous. He now had only 3,600 foot and 500 horse. Combined with the news that the Carlisle garrison had fallen to Cum-

berland this meant that an early return to England was impossible.

In Edinburgh Cumberland's bloodthirsty colleague General Henry 'Hangman' Hawley was erecting gibbets in the streets in anticipation of an early victory over the rebels. After all he had 8,000 troops at his disposal. Charles took the city of Stirling on 8 January and, reinforced by 6 pieces of heavy French artillery, laid siege to Stirling Castle. At Bannockburn on the 16th the Highland army waited for Hawley. When he did not materialise after two days Lord George Murray proposed occupying the high ground south of Falkirk. Hawley was taken so much by surprise by this brilliant move that, on 17 January, he was caught in his cups in the company of Lady Kilmarnock. In a ludicrous attempt to recover his composure he ordered his men to attack in the face of a blinding downpour. The dragoons were scattered by a Highland charge. The infantry, marching with the Glasgow Militia, suffered a similar fate at the hands of the Macdonalds. Hawley's reaction to losing 400 men (to a Jacobite figure of 40 dead) was to hang 31 of his own dragoons and shoot 32 of the infantry on charges of cowardice.

This latest Jacobite victory at

Continued on page 17

Falkirk so startled the British Government that Cumberland was sent north to deal with the situation. The Highland army might have prepared themselves to meet this egregiously unsuccessful soldier. Instead they wasted valuable time and effort in the siege of Stirling Castle while their prince, suffering from a cold, recuperated at Bannockburn House with his amorous nurse Clementina Walkinshaw. On 30 January Charles received a letter from the Highland chiefs recommending a retreat to their own territory. "Good God!", Charles raged, "have I lived to see this?" Yet he had to acquiesce because he had "an army that I cannot command any further than the chief officers please". He allowed himself one bitterly prophetic comment: "I wash my hands of the fatal consequences which I foresee but cannot help".

A dispirited Highland army began its retreat to Inverness on 1 February. Unlike the retreat from Derby this was a disorderly movement attended by farce. At Moy Hall, 16 miles from Inverness, Charles was entertained by young Lady Anne Mackintosh (whose husband was with the Government troops). Here an attempt by Lord Loudon's Hanoverian Highlanders to capture the Prince was averted by five men (led by the Moy blacksmith) simulating the noise of the entire Highland army. Loudon's men fled.

Pro-Jacobite Inverness was taken on 17 February. Two days later the Castle was captured and blown up. With headquarters at Culloden House Charles spent two months at Inverness putting on a brave front at balls and receptions. He had little to be happy about. The incident at Moy Hall, in which he had to venture outside in his night-clothes, had chilled him. His cold became pneumonia. More seriously, Government troops intercepted the Jacobite sloop *Prince*

*   *   *

Charles (a captured British ship renamed in his honour) bringing supplies and badly needed money—around £12,000—from France. From the south Cumberland was making a rapid advance and reached Nairn (on the Moray Firth, about 12 miles from Inverness) on 14 April.

Expecting an immediate attack the 6,000-strong Highland army gathered on Culloden Moor on 15 April. As hungry as they were their appetite for a fight was stronger. Cumberland did not come. He spent the day celebrating his 25th birthday at Nairn, giving his men brandy to drink his health. By contrast the Highlanders got one biscuit apiece on that day of anxious expectation.

Lord George Murray considered Culloden Moor totally unsuitable for Highland warfare. An open moor handed the advantage to Cumberland's powerful cavalry and long-range artillery. With unusual urgency Lord George proposed a night march on Nairn to give the Highlanders an opportunity to unleash a predawn charge on Cumberland's unsuspecting, hungover men. A delighted Charles authorised the plan which began after 8. With thirty Mackintoshes to guide him, Lord George led the Atholl Brigade. The prince followed with a second column. Heavy mist and a pitch-black night promised success.

History will never know what devastation a two-pronged Highland charge might have brought to Cumberland. The sluggishness of the rear column forced Lord George to delay at Kilvarock Castle, about half way to Nairn. It would be light before they reached the enemy. Sadly the Highlanders had to turn back towards Culloden Moor. When they got there some of them collapsed from hunger and exhaustion.

On Wednesday, 16 April 1745, the impossible happened—Cumberland advanced from Nairn. According to Charles's intelligence this was not even remotely likely. Nine thousand well-rested, well-fed, well-trained Government troops coming towards Culloden Moor. Two lines of red-coated infantry with fixed bayonets, flanked by cavalry with drawn sabres. There was even bagpipe music, supplied by the Campbell Militia.

The prince and his army were not ready for this assault. Confusion and thoughtlessness confounded weariness and lack of food. The Macdonalds were placed on the left-wing, although

they had been assured of a place on the right since the days of Bruce. There was no clearly formulated plan of attack. Charles did his best to restore morale by riding along his lines on a grey gelding. Dressed in a tartan coat and buff jacket he looked as splendid as ever. This time his men needed rest, money and provisions—not princely optimism.

It took Cumberland only 25 minutes to destroy the Highland army. On the open moor his artillery decimated the Jacobite ranks. Instead of charging immediately the Highlanders waited in the snow and sleet for Lord George's order. It was a long time coming. Recklessly the Mackintoshes made an unauthorised charge from the centre but were trapped by the Campbell Militia. When Lord George finally advanced, the firepower of the Hanoverian army proved too much for his men. It was a disaster. The dead lay four-deep. The wounded were butchered or left to a slow death. Some captured Highlanders were burned alive. Bodies were left on the Moor to rot, an early indication of Cumberland's methods of dealing with defiant clansmen.

Charles was reluctant to leave the battlefield, but O'Sullivan had other ideas. "All is going to pot!" he shouted, fleeing from the left wing. Then, grasping the bridle on Charles's horse, he dragged his Prince away. At the beginning of his venture Charles had boasted "I have taken a firm resolution to conquer or die, and to stand my ground as long as I shall have a man remaining with me". In the event he fled, and though he shed tears his "faithful Highlanders" were left to shed their blood and face a sustained period of quasi-genocidal oppression at the hands of "Butcher" Cumberland.

With a small mounted escort Charles rode westwards crossing the river Nairn at Faillie Ford. He picked up Edward Burke, a Gaelic-speaking Uist man as a guide, and dismissed his cavalry. At the house of Thomas Fraser of Gortuleg the prince met Lord Lovat for the first time. Whether he was really impressed by Lovat's advice to remain and regroup, Charles certainly authorised a letter to Cluny Macpherson promising to "pay Cumberland in his own coin" by gathering the clans at Fort Augustus with a scheme to make "ample amends for this day's ruffle". It may, on the other hand, have been a deliberate cover for

REBELL GRATITUDE,

a Representation of the Treachery and Barbarity of two Rebell Officers, at the Battle of Culloden, who had their Lives Generous-... by the Earl of Ancram, (Who had a considerable Command that Day) and by Captain Grosett Engineer & Aid De Camp to the Genera- ...he One attempted to shoot His Lordship behind his back with a Pistol, which He had kept concealed & which luckily only Flash'd in th- ...he Other Shot Captain Grosett Dead with his own Pistol, which happened Accidentally to fall from him as he was on Horseback, under pr- ...storing the same to the Captain. ———— These Rebells received the Just reward of their Perfidy By being immediatly cut to pieces by t- ...oops, And it is Generally believed that this their Ingratitude and Treachery greatly heightned the Slaughter that was that Day made o- ...ty.—— Captain Grosett left behind him a Destressed Widow, with Six young Children. —— This Battle was fought the 16 of April 1746. Publish'd According to Act of Parliament Jun.e 14 1747.

his actual intentions for Charles continued to move westwards and by 2 a.m. on Thursday reached the deserted Invergarry Castle where Ned Burke cooked salmon for him.

Next day the prince's little group rode to Glen Pean where they hoped to hear news of the army. The feeling was mutual. What remained of the Jacobite army, some 1,500 men, had gathered at Ruthven. Many felt deserted by the prince for whom they had risked so much. Lord George Murray in particular wrote an angry letter of resignation accusing the prince of incompetence for arriving without French help, and stupidity for relying on the likes of O'Sullivan who, Lord George contended, was hardly fit to look after luggage let alone an army. Charles, who had always been suspicious of Lord

George, was mortified. He sent a curt suggestion to Ruthven: "Let every man seek his safety in the best way he can". Personally he intended to escape.

Around five on the afternoon of 18 April Charles, Ned Burke, O'Sullivan, Father Allan Macdonald, and the Irish captain Felix O'Neil set off, on foot, over Glen Pean. From this decision dates the Prince's five months of wandering as a fugitive through the Western Highlands and Islands with a price of £30,000 on his head. Whatever criticisms may be levelled at Charles his own fortitude and stamina over the next five months are as amazing as they are admirable.

After the slog over Glen Pean the little group rested a day in a shieling on the Braes of Morar. At Borrodale Angus Macdonald's wife gave the

prince a new suit of Highland clothes and Angus himself hid the prince in the Beasdale woods. O'Sullivan persuaded the prince to seek the safety of the Long Island (the chain of outer Hebridean islands stretching from Barra Head to the Butt of Lewis) as they could count on the services of an excellent seaman, the 69-year-old Donald Macleod from Skye. Although Donald's first encounter with the prince was a refusal to seek the help of the lairds of Skye—who had, he maintained, "played the rogue"— Charles placed himself in the seaman's care. Donald's 61 days as the prince's pilot had a unique reward: he has been accorded a place on the Jacobite pantheon as The Faithful Palinurus.

In an eight-oared boat piloted by Donald, Charles and his four companions (Burke, O'Neil, O'Sullivan, Father Allan Macdonald) set off on the 70-mile journey to Benbecula on the night of Friday 25 April. By sheer luck all available ships had been sent to St. Kilda to look for Charles. It would have been a safe crossing had not a fearful storm lashed the boat so badly that Charles declared he would "rather face cannons and muskets". Donald and his 8-man crew steered them past Eigg and Rhum and on the 27th they reached Rossinesh on the east coast of Benbecula.

During his two months on the Long Island Charles was to be tested severely. From Fort Augustus Cumberland directed the search for the elusive prince. Savage men like captain Caroline Scott and captain John Fergusson patrolled the Minches and the Hebridean seas while Charles skulked about the rocky shores and thick heather moors waiting for a French ship. His movements took him as far south as Loch Boisdale, as far north as Stornoway. Living in caves, resting on heather, dashing up and down the wild coast hungry and damp and badly-clothed Charles never complained. Thus he achieved in his wanderings the kind of nobility he might never have known as a king.

On his way to Stornoway he stayed four days with the tenant of Scalpay, Donald Campbell, who, despite his name, accorded Charles perfect hospitality. The Presbyterian minister of Harris, Rev. Aulay Macaulay (great-grandfather of the Whig historian)

*   *   *

FACING PAGE: *'Rebell Gratitude', an anonymous engraving published in January 1747. This excuses Cumberland's savage reprisals by accusing the Highlanders of 'Treachery' and 'Barbarity'. According to the text the captured Highlander shot Captain Grosset dead with his own pistol. His 'just reward' was to be cut into pieces by the king's troops.*

RIGHT: *Simon Fraser, Lord Lovat (1667–1747). After crossing the Faillie Ford, Charles met Lovat at Gortelug House and was advised to remain in Scotland. In the event, Charles escaped but Lovat, who had spent a lifetime playing Whig against Tory advantages, was arrested and, on his way to trial and subsequent execution in London, he sat for Hogarth. He is seen counting the pro-Jacobite clans on his fingers.*

made an abortive attempt to capture Charles on Scalpay but dissolved at the prospect of a fight. At Stornoway the townspeople were incited against Charles by Rev. Macaulay so the prince had to sail to the uninhabited island of Iubhard. Ironically enough he might have been on his way back to France at this point: two French frigates had anchored at Borrodale on 3 May. In the absence of the prince they deposited about £38,000 worth of gold (which never reached Charles and which is supposedly still hidden at Loch Arkaig) before leaving with some prominent Jacobites, including Sheridan, and the dying Duke of Perth.

Any hopes of further refuge at Scalpay were dashed when it was

discovered that Donald Campbell had been forced into hiding. On their way to Benbecula the prince and his men narrowly escaped a government ship by lurking in shallow waters with only *dramach* (a mixture of meal and salt water) to sustain them. Eventually they reached Neil MacEachain Macdonald's property of Glen Corradale on the eastern side of South Uist. Here, in a forester's hut concealed between South Uist's two highest mountains, Charles spent three relatively idyllic weeks. From a cave above the hut he could even see the King's ships searching the Minch for him.

At Glen Corradale Charles passed his time fishing for cod and hunting grouse. Once, seeing a deer dart out

Continued on page 20

19

from the heather, he shot the animal. Ned Burke, detailed to butcher the animal, realised he was being watched by a cold, hungry boy. Burke struck the ogling child and was sharply rebuked by the Prince. "I cannot see a Christian perish for want of food and raiment had I the power to support them", Charles told Ned. True to his sentiments (which were fair enough in the circumstances) he shared some of the meat with the boy.

When he was not out hunting Charles received welcome gifts of whisky and brandy from the island gentry. It is probable that a reliance on drink during his cold fugitive months led to his dependence on it in exile. Neil MacEachain said "He took care to warm his stomach every morning with a hearty bumper of brandy, of which he always drank a vast deal, for he was seen to drink a whole bottle a day without being in the least concerned". His ability to hold his drink gave him the satisfaction of a minor victory in an all-night drinking marathon at Corradale. Swilling brandy out of sea-shells with a visiting group of Macdonalds Charles expatiated on the iniquity of European rulers. As the talk and drink flowed all the Macdonalds—even the hardened Boisdale—collapsed. Still on his feet, Charles covered the Macdonalds with their plaids and sang *De Profundis* for the good of their souls.

During their prince's hunting expeditions Colonel O'Neil and Neil MacEachain trudged through the green and brown and purple hills to study the movements of Government troops. O'Neil was particularly fond of the west side of the island where, at Milton, Flora Macdonald was over from Skye on a visit to her brother. His acquaintance with this attractive 23-year-old girl might have been cut short for, learning of a Government plan to land troops at each end of the Long Island with orders to meet at the middle, the Prince's party pressed south to Loch Boisdale. But Boisdale had been taken prisoner. Their predicament was terrifying.

Flora Macdonald's stepfather, Hugh Macdonald of Armadale, though a captain with the Government troops, was a clandestine Jacobite. He suggested the prince should seek refuge in Skye. So Charles, MacEachain and O'Neil set out for Milton and Flora while O'Sullivan and Father Allan Macdonald remained behind with the prince's baggage. On 20 June, having taken her brother's cattle to the pastures on Sheaval hill, Flora was asleep in a sheiling when she was

Continued on page 22

*   *   *

LEFT: *Flora Macdonald (1722–90). The 23-year-old Jacobite heroine who took the prince (disguised as 'Betty Burke'), 'over the sea to Skye'. She was the only daughter of Ranald Macdonald of Milton. On 12 July 1746, eleven days after leaving the prince at the Inn of Portree, Flora was arrested and eventually taken to the Tower of London. Released after the 1747 Act of Indemnity she returned to Scotland and married Allan Macdonald of Armadale. In 1774 they emigrated to America where her husband was captured at the battle of Moore's Creek in the American War of Independence. She returned to Scotland to die.*

FACING PAGE (above): *Mallaig Harbour where Charles landed on the mainland for the last time, after his wanderings in the islands. Later on 19 September 1746 he left Scotland for ever and began his long journey to France and Italy and a lonely exile that was to last until his death in 1787.*

FACING PAGE (below): *The 'Agreable Contrast', an engraving by W. Ebersley, 1746. A pro-Jacobite comparison of the prince and Flora to Cumberland and a town trollop. 'Shews that a Grayhound is more agreeable than an Elephant, & a Genteel personage More agreeably pleasing than a Clumsy one, a Country Lass is better than a town trollop and that Flora was better pleased than Fanny.'*

Pretender   Flora MacDonald   D. Cumberland   W. Ebenshey Inv.t et Sculp.t
1746

THE AGREABLE CONTRAST

ABOVE LEFT: *Princess Louise of Stol-berg. Conscious of a duty to produce a male heir, Charles married the 18-year-old princess in 1772; he was 52. The marriage produced no children and much distress for Charles and he took to drink; Louise took lovers. In 1780 she left Charles for the safety of a convent. Legal separation was declared in 1783 and Charles never saw her again.*

ABOVE RIGHT: *Prince Henry Benedict Stuart, duke of York and later cardinal York (1725–1807). In 1747 without consulting Charles, Henry left Paris to accept a cardinal's hat. This lessened still further the chance to produce a male Stuart heir and again identified the cause with Catholicism. After Charles's death Henry assumed the title Henry IX and amassed a large fortune, but was financially ruined during the Napoleonic occupation of Italy in 1799. George III took pity on him and awarded him an annual pension of £4,000. When he died in 1807, the male line of the House of Stuart became extinct.*

RIGHT: *Charlotte, duchess of Albany (1735–89). After his separation from Louise, Charles legitimised his only daughter as duchess of Albany in 1784. She comforted him in his few remaining years and he lavished gifts and money on her. Charlotte became the mistress of archbishop Ferdinand de Rohan and had three children. She survived her father by little more than a year.*

wakened by MacEachain and, as she later put it in her third-personal account of the adventure, "went out as fast as she could throw on some of her cloaths". She listened to O'Neil's proposal that she should obtain a pass to Skye from her stepfather and take the prince dressed as a servant-girl. On the grounds that it would implicate her friends and compromise her reputation she refused. O'Neil whistled. Prince Charles emerged from behind the hut. Flora's objections crumbled.

Deciding on Rossinesh as a meeting-place, the prince, O'Neil and MacEachain went up the east coast while Flora kept to the west. Conveniently arrested by her stepfather Flora obtained a personal pass to Skye plus a letter explaining the existence of "one Betty Burke, an Irish girl". Betty Burke was, of course, Bonnie Prince Charlie.

Flora now acted with firm resolve. She refused to let O'Neil come as his existence was unexplained. She also told Charles to leave his pistols with O'Neil as they would give him away in a search. "Indeed, Miss", Charles replied, "if we happen to meet with any that will go that narrowly to work in searching me as what you mean they will certainly discover me at any rate". Flora was adamant, so, with only a cudgel for protection Charles put on his quilted petticoat, his blue and white gown, and his hooded cloak to become Betty Burke. At 8 a.m. on 28 June they were ready to leave.

The open boat that took the prince "over the sea to Skye" was 18 feet long and had a helmsman and four oarsmen in addition to Flora, "Betty", and Neil MacEachain. Charles was cheerful enough to sing Flora to sleep with *The King shall enjoy his own again* though reality contradicted the sentiments of the song. At Vaternish, the north-west wing of Skye, the boat was spotted by Government troops. At Mugstot, home of Sir Alexander Macdonald, Government officers were enjoying island hospitality. Charles had to make his way, on foot, to Portree. There, at a small inn, he said good-bye to Flora: "For all that has happened, I hope, Madam, we shall meet at St. James's yet and I will reward you there for what you have done". Then, with a bottle each of whisky and brandy tied to his belt, he sailed to the narrow island of Raasay to spend two nights in a hut. It was too dangerous to remain on

Raasay so, disguised as Lewie Caw, a manservant, he returned to Skye and walked 24 miles over wild countryside to Elgol. He was in Mackinnon country and in good hands. Admirers gave him a banquet in a cave near Port na Cullaidh and provided a boat to take him to the Scottish mainland. He landed at Mallaig around 4 a.m. on 5 July.

Now the attempts to capture the prince intensified. It took considerable ingenuity and the help of Angus Macdonald of Borrodale (whose home had been burned) to put the prince in contact with Alexander Macdonald of Glenladale. The countryside round Arisaig was swarming with redcoats yet, with all the evasive expertise now at his command, Charles reached the Braes of Glenmoriston on 24 July and for thirty days enjoyed the protection of the Men of Glenmoriston, a Highland guerilla group. He moved through rain and sleet, across hills and heather, to Badenoch. By now he was barefoot, bearded, and dressed in a philabeg and old shirt. On 29 August he reached the north-east slope of Benalder and, next day, met Lochiel. Recognising his prince Lochiel made to kneel in homage. Charles, with the insight of a fugitive rather than a prince, stopped him. "Oh no, my dear Lochiel, you don't know who may be looking from the tops of yonder hills". When Lochiel invited him to a meal of mutton, beef, butter and cheese Charles was so overwhelmed he commented "Now, gentlemen, I live like a prince". Not quite. His next home was not a palace but Cluny Macpherson's cave on the southern slope of Benalder. In Cluny's Cage (familiar to readers of R. L. Stevenson's *Kidnapped* where it is described as "a nest upon a cliff-side") he hid until 13 September when the news of two French privateers in Loch nan Uamh shifted him. Covering the 100 miles to the coast within a week he boarded *l'Heureux* at Borrodale. On 20 September 1746 he left Scotland for ever.

In his wake he left Highland Scotland to experience unprecedented persecution. Disarming acts deprived Highlanders of their weapons and even their distinctive dress. In comparison with this cultural tragedy Charles's own decline in exile was merely pathetic. Like his father he became a lost cause but, unlike James, he could not admit it. In Paris he threatened Lord George. When his

brother accepted a cardinal's hat he ignored him for 18 years. Banished from France by the 1748 Treaty of Aix-la-Chapelle he took a house opposite the Louvre and struck his own medal. It was all posturing. He was arrested on his way to the opera, imprisoned until he agreed to leave France, and sent on his way to Avignon. Even on Papal territory he was not safe, for the British, holding that Avignon was on French soil, threatened to bombard the port of Rome unless he left. Charles thereafter continued his wanderings on a European scale.

In 1750 he visited London, *incognito,* and was received into the Anglican church. A year later the failure of the Elibank Conspiracy (a plot to capture the Hanoverian Royal Family) plunged him further into alcoholic despair. Clementina Walkinshaw came from Scotland to be his mistress and presented him with a daughter, Charlotte, in 1753. Far from bringing him happiness the child became another source of friction between Charles and Clementina.

He felt isolated among enemies. Even an offer to lead an attack on Minorca (on the outbreak of the Seven Years War in 1757) could not tempt him. His sardonic refusal was "I will no longer serve as a mere bugbear". The Coronation of George III in 1760 was a painful date for him. While the House of Hanover settled permanently into his rightful kingdom Prince Charles Edward Stuart was not even master of his own lodgings. That year Clementina took his daughter away to a convent. Not only had they disagreed over the education of Charlotte but Clementina claimed to live "in perpetual dread of my life" from the Prince's "violent passions".

The fact that James had sanctioned Clementina's desertion of him further embittered him against his father. It was only the Old Pretender's imminent death in 1766 that brought him to Rome. Even then he arrived too late. The king (of the Jacobites) was dead: the *de jure* king had another 22 years to endure. Cardinal York's attempts to have Charles III recognised by the pope failed, but reconciled the two brothers. Charles recovered some of his old panache and entered Roman society as Count Albany. He even took up shooting again.

Increasingly conscious of a duty to produce a Stuart heir (in view of his brother's celibacy) Charles married in

IACOBO · III
IACOBI · II · MAGNAE · BRIT · REGIS · FILIO
KAROLO · EDVARDO
ET · HENRICO · DECANO · PATRVM · CARDINALIVM
IACOBI · III · FILIIS
REGIAE · STIRPIS · STVARDIAE · POSTREMIS
ANNO · M·DCCC·XIX

BEATI MORTVI
QVI IN DOMINO MORIVNTVR

1772, at the age of 52. He was financially and physically unable to satisfy his 19-year-old wife, princess Louise of Stolberg, so while they drifted about Italy she took lovers and he took more brandy. There were no children. Louise retired to a convent in 1780 with the blessing of the pope and half Charles's annual pension. Fortunately for Charles a legal separation was arranged in 1783.

A year later his only daughter came to live with him. He had Charlotte legitimised as duchess of Albany, and she humoured her father and protected him from the unbearable memories of 1745. By 1787 he was serene enough to return to the Palazzo Muti and the Roman Catholic faith. One year later, after a paralytic stroke, he died. His brother buried him at Frascati, his own cathedral. In 1807 his remains were removed to Rome and buried in the crypt of St. Peter's.

Though he survived for almost 70 years he had virtually *lived* only one: *Bliadna Thearlaich*, Charlie's Year, that 18-month period from 25 July, 1745, to 19 September, 1746 when, against overwhelming odds, and with only the conviction of his own courage he had almost achieved the impossible. Failing to win a crown, he gained immortality. Bonnie Prince Charlie's legend of elegant courage has effortlessly outlived the House of Stuart.

★   ★   ★

LEFT: *Antonio Canova's marble monument to the Stuarts, in St. Peter's Basilica, Rome. It was paid for by George III and erected in 1819. The last three male Stuarts carved on the monument are buried in the crypt of St. Peter's.*

★

ACKNOWLEDGMENTS

With the exception of the following, all the illustrations in this book are reproduced by permission of the Scottish National Portrait Gallery; The Royal Collection, pp i cover, 12/13, 16, by gracious permission of H.M. The Queen; pp 5, 21 (top), Laird Parker of Oban; p 2 (top left), by permission of the Trustees of Blairs College; p 6, by permission of Colonel D. H. Cameron of Lochiel; pp 6 (bottom), 14 (top right), Radio Times Hulton Picture Library; p 7, by permission of the Duke of Atholl; p 8 (bottom), 9, Peter Baker, Clevedon; p 10, Thomas Coram Foundation; p 11, British Tourist Authority; pp 8 (top), 14 (top left and bottom), 15, J. Pugh, A.I.I.P., A.R.P.S.; pp 19, 22 (top right), National Portrait Gallery, London; p 21 (bottom), by permission of the Trustees, British Museum; p 24, Mansell Collection.

SBN 85372 163 7   173/40